SPACES OF SIGNIFICANCE:
AN OFF THE CHEST POETRY ANTHOLOGY

CW01454681

Off The Chest has been creating spaces for poetry since 2019. Formed by poets Iftikhar Latif and Ella Dorman-Gajic, our mission is to give a platform to poets of diverse backgrounds and celebrate original voices in the UK poetry scene. We do this by holding poetry events and workshops across England and online. We are proudly supported by Arts Council England. You can find out more about our upcoming events and workshops at offthechest.co.uk

ISBN: 978-1-916938-91-5

Cover designed by Cia Mangat

Edited by: Jake Wild Hall and Aaron Kent

Typeset by Aaron Kent

Broken Sleep Books Ltd
PO Box 102
Llandysul
SA44 9BG

Spaces of Significance

Edited by
Aaron Kent and Jake Wild Hall

Curated with
Ella Dorman-Gajic and Iftikhar Latif

Broken Sleep Books

CONTENTS

A piece of Off The Chest you can hold in your hands? Hell yeah!

We began Off The Chest from a shared passion for poetry spaces.

In fact, it was at an open mic where we (Iftikhar and Ella) first met. Our plan began on a whim, and soon we organised a night of poetry in the back of the HiLand Café in Mile End, East London. Since then, we've filled spaces far and wide; our open mic events have spanned multiple venues in London and other cities such as Leeds and Brighton. Each event offers the chance for members of our audience to perform their poems as part of the open mic, and boy do they deliver! The nature of the open mic means we never know what we're going to get; but one thing is for sure – our poets never fail to serve up explosive words and wisdom, stories and ideas, laughter and poignancy. We're proud to say that we've also welcomed feature-length sets from highly acclaimed poets, such as Yomi Ṣode, Cecilia Knapp, Kareem Parkins-Brown, Joe Carrick-Varty, Jasmine Gardosi, Sanah Ahsan and Rachel Long, plus many more. We have also organised workshops to support the craft of writing poetry. Our workshops have been facilitated by the likes of Ella Frears, Anthony Anaxagorou, Lewis Buxton and many more legendary poets.

Many people tend to come up to us after one of our events or workshops and ask how we got started, how long we have been running for and how special these spaces make them feel. But we'd like everyone to know that you can do it too. Spaces for creativity and community can be made by anyone, and nurtured with some planning, time and passion. Although we have received funding, we began on a shoestring fuelled by the kindness of café owners who gave us a space for free. That was so long as we worked out how to fit 50 people into their tiny backroom, without accidentally falling into the audience's laps (...and there were some close calls). We have even had events where only a handful of people showed up, but those events were just as special as the spaces where we've entertained 100+ audience members. Why? Because spending just a few hours with people in a space where they can share their writing always brings people closer together, which is something special.

Despite the growing number of people around us, our world feels increasingly fragmented, and people can often struggle to find community. Poetry, performed in a live space, is a powerful force. It allows us to share experiences, helps us build empathy and, ultimately, form friendships and foster communities.

And what about this anthology? Consider this book a collection of love letters, explorations, and accounts of spaces which are significant to our poets. Our motto has always been to create spaces for poetry, but poetry exists in endless spaces. Whether that's on a grotty London bus, or in the depths of the ocean. The significance of each space in this series of poems is unique, and we are so proud to have collated these exceptional voices in Off The Chest's first-ever anthology.

Thank you so much for spending your time in these spaces. We hope you enjoy reading.

With love,
Ella Dorman-Gajic and Iftikhar Latif

Founders of Off The Chest

THIS IS THE AGE OF SELF-REFLECTION; NEVER WILL ANYONE BE AS INTERESTED IN ME AS I AM. Once, standing on the pedestrian bridge next to the A814, I saw a kingfisher fly across the Kelvin. Unmistakable colours, streak of marigold and turquoise like a west coast sea, the brightest thing I've ever observed in nature. So I called everyone who would care, everyone who would care to receive a call from me about a bird I'd seen, and of course this could only be my parents, who said, *how wonderful; you will never see anything like that in your life again*, and I thought about how for the longest time humans lived in caves, never had any cause to change, and the generations of sameness, the generations of stillness. We're out now but often I'll stand by the dual carriageway under an overhang of pine where sounds of trains and cars and lorries chase each other into a constant and the sap is a hereditary olfactory memory, and for a moment I imagine everything that exists is enough now, the endless knocking down and digging up and re-laying and covering over can stop. But I would miss the peace of hearing too much at once, the sound of travelling too fast headlong into a serene oblivion. The caves must have been so quiet, nothing but us, repeating and reflecting; what determined torture. Where the dual carriageway crosses the Kelvin, and the Kelvin meets the Clyde, at low tide there is often a heron wading up the riverbed, and every spring I've ever seen here since I've been here a swan nests on the slipway that looks towards Govan. Such irrepressible genetic legacies. I stop children in their tracks and say *you will never see anything like that in your life again*.

THE ENDS
After Caleb Femi

two girls in the club toilet
reapplying Rimmel lipstick in shade 'scandalous'
talking about posting thirst traps on Instagram
the way a country plans for war
at the afters, they pass the spliff back and forth
fingers reaching
             like a Michelangelo painting

a lighter thief
comes home from the party
lines up Clippers of all colours on a shelf
decides that from now on
he'd rather use a matchbox instead

the girl who wears Air Force 1s
under her shalwar kameez at the function
she smirks at her tiny victory
her mother shakes her head

youts trading Match Attax
in the playground like it's Wall Street
the bendy 18 bus as an after school motive

God in the corner shop
buying Raws and a Magnum
as he leaves, he says
when people die, you get left
with all the admin

the girl who dreams of getting married
walking down a Wetherspoon's carpet
holding newspapered chips
like a bouquet of flowers
in a sari that used to be her mother's
the mother is happier
on her daughter's wedding day
than she was on her own

men at the barge
sculpt coat hooks out of their sadness
all of the ills of childhood whittled
and sanded and varnished
from the street window you can see
a father's absence
eating sandwiches by the telly

LOVE SONG ON THE M4

Last night I tucked my head into the familiar hollow
of your shoulder and said *do you still want me now*

I'm old because we're driving to the airport just us
and in the mirror I see the battle

between gravity and my cheeks is on
the turn. We used to drive around at eighteen

singing *stay, if you wanna love me,*
stay and you would tap the tambourine

part on the wheel while I watched
your beautiful neck. That's the sort of thing

I thought back then, tense boomerang
of longing, that no one in the world had ever had

a neck like yours. The song comes on, road bronzed
with October trees, bright lampposts, light so heavy

it lands like benediction. Surely at eighty-eight
I'll think of this enamelled morning, the first

few grey hairs lit up at your temples. You tap
the tambourine part on the wheel like always,

it was always *stay, if you wanna*
and I did, that's the marvel of it, yes, I did.

23ᴿᴰ MARCH

today i spent thirty minutes reading a substack about bird songs and how spending time learning to tell them apart is a way to boycott the attention economy. in that time, elon musk earned more than half a million pounds. men with awful egos can invent cars that explode and drive into traffic, but there is still not a phone that can capture what it's like to look at the moon, or the sunset. a video on my timeline shows people stepping over a deliveroo driver collapsed on the ground in the front of their building. migrant children making hot cheetos report that the spicy dust makes their lungs sting. i never feel my own lungs and i never want to. you can grow onions from onions, and plant garlic to grow garlic. each clove a potential mother. what would happen if i planted the thoughts i have as i scroll on my phone, or pushed my commute time under wet soil, or seeded this moment, right now. sometimes i want to, when i am lying next to you. you falling asleep in record time, and me wanting to stay awake just to hold onto this, whatever it is. my speech therapist would tell me to hold my breath in, and hold it, and imagine my words battling to get out, knocking at my lips, and let go, let go, let go

DID YOU HEAR THE ONE ABOUT THE TWO YOUNG BROWN MEN
After Wayne Holloway-Smith

who pretended not to be lovers on the bus
how it was the only option to avoid fatalities
so one of them sat far away on a priority seat
cause he could never stomach the sight of his
lover walking away from him for the final time
so sat next to a daddima with a beige coat that was
sprinkled with droplets of mango juice stains
who rambled on about losing her teeth to coke
while he tried to hide his mulberry plump eye
he dared not turn back to see his baby boy
in case someone sniffed out the acrid smoke
emanating from the body of a forbidden lover
who just wants to make it home safely tonight
and beforeyouknowitbloodshriekedeverywhere
and beforeyouknowitaslurislodgedinthebrain
that is how they become memories an inside voice
he watched two men holding hands enter the bus
they giggled all the way up to the top deck and
then stopped to smack lips moaned and moaned
unsurprisingly nobody really cared about them
because white skin was a default for tolerance
a shield cloak acceptance escape from brutality
the daddima said they looked so happy together
then babbled on about her settling in England
the man next to her with a tear that tore him said
what if they were two brown men kissing like them
thebusterminatedduetoafaultyengine

CARVERY

See all the windows are plainly crying
met cold with best Sundays' steam.
With the millions who escaped reduction —
they'd rather blur their reluctant contact
than let out all the rising stock to the wind
and serve up clouds to the undeserving set.

This barrel you now inhabit is holding you safe,
in its securely wound and vicing iron band,
from an inner warm embrace that can't escape.
While about as rolled full as you're willing to get,
and still dreaming of that tender middle slice,
some voice whispers 'you're not beaten yet'.

And now we too are backwards sinking,
to relive those hazel meaty juice-doused days,
in all life's journaled festive gatherings,
with our glory glazed seasoned fill, well dressed.
And though not a patch on the real quilted stuff,
we're still testing how absorbent we might get.

Too full to care - we doff our sunken suet caps.
On homely nasal fog, whistle and breathe in the safety
of temporary housing, as back up for seconds we stand.
It's about as close as we're ever striving to get.
Consoling with some cast-out honeyed gristle.
And hoping neither of us win the bet.

BATHTUB
after Casey Smith and Fresh

I want to be the girl in the bathtub / at a party
whose forehead you're touching
I want someone to move my hair
out of my eyes wide and seabright

I want to be the girl in the bathtub / at a party
who's wearing the cutest crop top
refracting in the water / rising
up to my soft throat / my sharp jaw

I want to be wearing seafoam green
I think I'd like it to be summer
I'd like it to be a dinner party
I'd like to be making small talk

everyone wants a simple answer
I want to be snakebite drunk in the bathtub
I want to dive / I want to be sea / snake / bite /
a shoal of bumphead parrot fish

a shoal / a mess of human teeth
take chunks out of skin / divers /
pearls at the tips of fingers
I want to be human teeth drunk

I am valued / I am loved
I am allergic to the soapsuds
the bathwater / I am developing a rash
on my back all barnacles / limpet / bivalve

I am wearing a crop top / I am lying
on the cold tiles of your posh bathroom
I am letting the cold / your hand / seep into me
I am a cold pool / you are touching my forehead

WILDFLOWERS

That lazy maple syrup sun pours slow
across the evening; you lay a liver-
spotted palm in mine on the patio
as bees dance boleros in the border
hedge. Deckchair-stretched, the tender sunset wind
laps at your ponytail, your wicker
threaded hat; daydreamed star of imagined
cola ads. Our flowing wildflowers

wave away years: once we were thirty-one,
grubby-palmed, planting new-leaved seedpaper –
those first fresh daisies & dandelions

for this place we made to grow together.
Darling, the very heavens aren't as precious
as this small patch of good earth we call ours.

CODEC // MERYL (ARMORY)
After 'Metal Gear Solid' by Hideo Kojima & Tomokazu Fukushima

& each camo suit

   had a name.

My greengilled riflefire bled

   those polygons,

exitwounded

   their lives in one cathode ray

frame. How many ka/has must be

   cleft before a new-

born's forefinger wears the snug

   crease of a trigger? When dawn

sings in her first snow

   drifts, I hope our guns

have saved more lung-

   heaves than they stilled. North,

a lone ice crevasse craves

   to touch the terse bite

of your boots. Go, my queasy tongue

   might then taste clean.

We, both of us, have canyons

   we must cross tonight.

MY LOVE'S A HOUSE

My love's a house I can't afford. The price
   Of my love, indebted and unbrokered,
Is infinite. High windows, flowers, no mice
   In sight to nibble at your drawers. I heard
You sing in the kitchen once. There's an island
   For cocktails on the rocks, where you are free
   To sing your songs and make a wretch of me.
We'll prosper in this house of love. I've planned
   A party, to ensure it's warm, in the kitchen
With the island, in a place we dream to share.
   Our friends, taken, when we invite them in,
Will say—What a beautiful house!—What a thing
Is love, that returns more love, with love to spare!

NAMING THINGS

That's oak, you'll say. Or is it sycamore?
I roll my eyes, as you (the parent) name
Them: conker and copter, shoestring war
Games, *beigoma* spun off morning telly
Shows about 'bit beasts' dormant within
Objects. Waked by motion, they ripcord
From extended arms into wide open air
To collide like British bulldogs at break-
Time outside class. Wars were old news,
First or second period. I had Stronghold
Crusader for PC. Drag-and-drop troops,
Point-and-click war machines. I'd mouth
Ballista like a Sunday league casualty—
And knew holy war by Maths homework
At the St Peter's Primary I was loathe to
Outgrow, much like the Hitchean mantra
That god is not great (he's probably OK,
If that's your kettle of fish). My old man
Taught me to cast a line at Upper Bittell.
An angler, he said, will squeeze a maggot
To hook it for bait, piercing the arse-end
As the wormings' curling finger beckons
Its little nub when pinched. I was seven.
Lord of the Rings: The Two Towers had
Hit cinemas; the ozone was still burning.
Across the reservoir a tree with a plaque
Grows up, our name in mind. I forget its
Name in return. I knew it once, I promise,
And I'm sorry I don't call enough. I drop

The line through blank air—an inimitable
Thing hanging from it. Were I forbidden,
A pilgrim with no passport to that place
I can no longer return, I, too, would travel
To the centre of the earth to bring back
What's lost, before all is. Today the news
Is in my mouth. *I'll be with you, whatever*
I say, the right words gone from us. I hope
No one reads this. I'll be damned if they
Bring up how devastated I am when I say
I love you, how lost our joy is, how alone.

THE HOUSE BLEW UP

The family act
like it's a normal evening.

I'm flapping clammy hands,
too aware of the ticking in the basement.

We cannot just evacuate like hysterics,
Dad says, *we must do things properly.*

The dining room is laid out for the sake of the table,
the people an afterthought, squeezed

between wood and wall, not enough space
to get out quickly when the time comes.

Dad cooks. He's the only one
who can be trusted.

Well, says Mum, setting food down, *last meal
before, duh-duh duh duh duuuh!*

She gives a hint of jazz hands, puts on a dramatic voice, as if
the impending explosion were an amateur play starring one of us.

As usual Dad and Jack, who has just discovered
communism, argue about politics. As usual

I remain silent. *Half an hour to go
and we haven't even done the dishes,* says Mum.

Dad asks why I'm sulking.
I tell him I'm not.

You always say that when you're sulking.
What is it now?

The clock ticks.
I know it's wrong to be scared.

One minute to go. Mum is still
doing the dishes, singing to herself.

I hold in a scream. One second.
Dad looks at me, waiting for an answer.

THE CLOSET

I pull my grandfather's khaki suit trousers
over my hips. They are light linen,
the type he would wear back in St Vincent.
He embraces me in the snap of the waist.
When I push my hand into the right pocket
I find
a pink handkerchief with a burgundy trim.
When I push my hand into the left pocket
I find
a betting slip
squeezed and oiled by fingertips.
Fears rolled up in receipts.
A remembering,
an odd habit,
a worry toy.
Our fingers meet again
index thumb middle.

He wore a tie every day, glint
of gold from his filled in gap.
When I smile I glint gold too.
My grandmother hates it,
although she loved it on him.

UNIFORM

Sticky floor, slouched beanie,
mohawk galore, black skinny jeans,
tattered, frayed at the seams,
and a thick glossy layer of black, smothering eyelids.
Brick heavy boots and zebra stripes,
dull lit rooms and flashing lights –
rhythmic chants and melodic basslines,
band t-shirts, and crowded frenzies.
Factory-made prototype world,
shared visions and beliefs
in a transcendent power.
Swaying and moving to its call.

Sun-drenched paths and tropical green,
flooding every inch of land the eye can see.
Cotton shirts and sandal shoes,
baggy *pyjama* greets the deluge.
Monsoon rain on the rooftop,
hiding from mosquitos in the open air.
3 boys stand at the back of a truck.
A man in a *lunghi* rides a motorbike at dawn.
At 11 o'clock, a tea stall is set up on the roadside.
It is break time, and men can be seen
flocking to the makeshift establishment
for tea and cigarettes, *paan* and conversation,
looking for gossip and fuel
to face another day's work.
Their mothers and wives are adorned in patterned designs,
embroidered cotton scarves and *shalwar kameez*,

flowing in the midday breeze.
A loose *dupatta* hangs over strands of hair,
seen in braids or plaits or summer frizz.
The scene is overlaid by the sound of the *adhan*,
echoing from a nearby minaret.

"*Hayya'alas-Salah. Hayya'alas-Salah.*"
Bearded men in pristine white robes
converge at the entrance of the masjid.

"*Hayya'alal-Falah. Hayya'alal-Falah.*"
A crowd forms, denting the surface with synchronized movements,
following learnt motions,
bowing and raising head and limbs.

A loud cymbal sounds.
Everyone is still.
A gentle melody begins, reverberating from a single electric guitar.
The swarm of people release a thunderous applause,
nodding and gesticulating their excitement.
Scanning the bodies, faces unrecognisable in the darkness,
the souls populating this room,
one can observe a baseline fact.
That they have arrived at this venue
in search of music and revelry,
nostalgia and conversation,
head-banging through the evening,
looking for respite and purpose
to face another day's work.

Standing together, shoulder to shoulder.
The men in white offer their *namaz,*

their prayers to the Most High,
kneeling and bowing,
forehead to the ground in unison,
they whisper sacred lines
and point to a holy land.
They hold within them
shared visions and beliefs,
in a transcendent power,
moved by His call.

There can be found, among community,
shared perspectives and identity,
a deep sense of belonging and trust,
common understanding of this *dunya* — this reality,
and a discernible uniformity.

Being called to a place of joy and togetherness
is part of the fabric of human life,
a tender longing
to feel a part of something
greater than ourselves.
It is this which drives us,
wherever we may be,
from East to West,
from land to sea,
from cluttered temples to outdoor fields,
from concert halls to prayer mats on the motorway,
from sacred walls to basement rooms,
from theatres and stadiums,
to towering structures
built in the name of sacred scripture.

There is a deep longing for connection.
Found among slouched beanies and dip-dyed hair,
skinny black jeans and netted tights.
Shalwar kameez and flowing veils,
baggy *pyjamas* and thick beards.
It is all uniform.

VIGILANTES, AFTER HOURS

We watch Scorsese in 35mm, Tamil drooling lips
of Truffle linguine. A man is trapped in papier-mâché,

and I can't help thinking of the puffer coat swollen
to the size of a bouncy castle in couture.

Somewhere, a boat capsizes hundreds from Pakistan,
Syria, Palestine. Elsewhere – a submarine.

Here we are, watching Scorsese loop
the night, while the sun implodes over London's skyline.

Later, I swing my bag on someone and do not apologise.
The buskers play Gulzar, *chaiyya chaiyya chaiyya* –

Oh, the price of *Americanos*! *these days*, Oh,
the price of billboards on Tottenham Court Road!

Yesterday, in the "land of gems", two women
and a child are burnt alive. Soldiers hold vigil.

Over limoncello spritz, we speak of America's
westward bulldozing over our people.

This year Schiaparelli throws out measuring-tape
belts, and Scorsese throws out film.

It's easier to shoot at night, that way.
Beneath frescoes of the Petit Palais, a keyhole

is sliced to frame a woman's belly button.
I burn myself with a hot water bottle, and it scars

to the shape of a map. In the hills and valleys,
people bleed into Burma. *It's not time to forget.*

There are many names for what we do, Scorsese
says, as we gently papier-mâché before bed.

I WRITE GHAZALS, THEY WRITE CODE IN SILICON VALLEY
THIS GHAZAL IS AN ODE
for Silicon Valley,

What is better than porn and worms
haunting your hard drive? A poem.

Forgotten verses, they roam and byte,
then we commit to archive a poem.

Distil a ghazal from a data lake,
storm the clouds to revive a poem.

Mine coins until the oceans are burning,
& there is no longer a way to survive a poem.

How sweetly bonds bloom with each coded
couplet, [ransom a stanza to derive a poem.]

O binary melodies! O syntax of singing loops!
A Sufi's rules need not deprive a poem.

Dissolve in this democracy of generative bards —
who am I, a mere mortal, to chastise a poem?

Yes, this cosmos of code may quip and rhyme,
but could androids ever learn how to jive a poem?

In Silicon Valley they teach ghazals to code,
How else will they know they are alive? *#A poem.*

HOME FOR COOPERATION

Just outside the window, barbed wire glints
in the midday sun. A United-Nations-white
canopy shades a United-Nations-white car.

In this UN Buffer Zone, the English
language unites fifteen writers from Cyprus,
Belarus, Greece, Lebanon, Palestine, Syria,
and the United Kingdom.

Laptops are tapped, like typewriters
once would have been when Britain wrote
the constitution for this island.
Pens scribble frantically with a seven-minute time limit.

When the bell chimes noon,
there are still two new poems to be shared.
No one says they need to leave,
although many have driven far to be here,
and two have flights to catch this afternoon.

Two lads from London and Athens will leave
Cyprus queerer than when they arrived
five days ago. Decades ago. Centuries ago.

Outside the Home for Cooperation, fifteen writers
gather for a photo. They'll tag each other
on social media. Stay connected. Reach out. Return
or accept follows and requests of friendship.

YOU HAVE BEEN WALKING THE RELIC TRAIN TRACK BACK TO KRAGUJEVAC
For Deda

when, at twenty-seven, you reach it:
the church of Deda's childhood
... you'd forgotten the dress code.
Wrap your Nike T-Shirt around your hair.
Molim... molim? You attempt to ask a nun
for her spare skirt, when Sveti Nikola's
eyes lock yours and suddenly

you are seven years old,
Deda is pressing Sveti Nikola to your palm
until he leaves a mark. You hear the psalms
he chants; you know about the train; he asks
Jel idemo u Kragujevac? So you nod, yes...
really, you know only one word in his tongue: *sedi*
meaning: *sit down* — you, always running far away.

But at twenty-seven, you have run here:
to stand on the ghost
of his footprint, the balcony he sang from.
You light a candle, feel it judge your unholy
hands. From above, Deda watches
its flame plume through the church doors
down the railway line, across Kragujevac —

in his final moments, Deda sang lost psalms
into an empty carriage. Train tracks
pulled up at the edge of a map.
British mash on his lips, yet the only

language left within was that of his
childhood — a time before seventy
years parted his voice from his walls.

Deda boarded his train back to Kragujevac.
Each day, it pulls up at his station, with-
out a body inside. Deda boarded a train
to Kragujevac. Until the day he died,
he was waiting to get off.
Jel idemo u Kragujevac?

Are we going home?

HALF FULL

It is the summer you watch
the girls crash into the lido.
Your bikini cups half full,
mouths absent of your name. All year,
you'd sat next to a boy in geography.
Today, he walks across the knife
edge of pool. When he reaches your
eye, turns his head to the lads, jokes
crackling, their apples dropping
into the girls' wet palms.

If Jen sneaks up behind you,
unties your bikini — the faintest touch —
and calls your name, then you,
fuelled with faux courage,
will run towards the water.
Oh... now they look, arrows
for fingers, whites of eyes. Burning
blisters into your bare chest
is not the sun's smoulder
but the laughter,
as they watch it fall.

DRINK IN THE CITY

sniff the fat fresh cut grass
in the park with pink blossoming
trees every corner and children!
children screaming heads off
in dandelion joy the air is plugged
with warm rays of energy crashing over
us in waves of laughter, of clawing
ecstasy i haven't felt this in me
since late last summer when you
told me you loved me just like
you thought it was a known secret
and i, ever the genius, ignored it
because i was

                                    held tight
by the blankets, sinking in
it was warm golden custard
served with rainbow
-sprinkled school cake with
each dripping spoon shovelling
angel dust and the first bite
tasted just as good as the last
bite and every bite in between
was skydiving into sweetness
backflips into buttery folds
powdered sugar sheets
ever since then i've been

hooked to the taste
and this city
baby,
it's ours,
all ours

RECORDING WANDSWORTH COMMON ON AN ANNIVERSARY

In the park, hectic, heist the squirrels,
to ethereal strains of the theme
to Mission Impossible, syncopated
and overlaid in synaptic noise,
more enlivening than the sticky silence,
this message will self-destruct...

In the park, I am a pencil mark of a promise,
waiting for echoes, on our favourite bench,
in memorial, brave facing the sunset,
for the grave, kept secret I am telling,
with wild whistling insouciance of an unwatched pot,
undercover at the dead drop, dropped hot
for collecting images as instructions,
boiling, this blood is a heist of squirrels.

In the park, a thought from a source
that can be trusted, open air is closer
to verdant shadows, their shoots swaying
sultry dappled greens, fizzing with residuals.
You always loved squirrels.
And it settles, an ever-cooling memory
from the Horrendous Space Kablooie,
from your entropy moving through, churning
particles in my tape machine, mechanical
chewing of scenery, stage whispering my mission.

And I sit there for hours,

Until I choose to accept it,

All white noise, is EVP, is you.

And this message will self-destruct...

DEAR DIARY, I MET DESIRE TODAY.

Found some roadside jewellery the same colour
as her birth moon and wore it like a lottery ticket.
She's up on the podium getting awards,
telling other writers their work is 'getting better.'
Now, every time she pauses, a guy checks on her
as she retches on flowerbeds, our moment near.
In my hand, a post-it note says 'she's with me,'
trying to act mature, wondering if she wants
me the same. She's a known lover-girl,
just not mine. Coffee percolates before sunrise,
our arms diverge like anxious drivers.
It makes sense when our MRI scans are together,
but when she disappoints, it's never completely
contextualised. She ghosted me on bin collection day.
"I didn't drag you to the base of this fear" I said.
Air cracks with sexual tension, bringing down
the bridge. "This isn't romance, I got swept up
by your chaos." A full fridge told the cook,
"Don't tell me you're overwhelmed,
you've wanted this for weeks."

CLEARING YOUR CHEST

I box up beta blockers from your chest
of drawers dentures knee brace Nicorette gum

three unopened letters from Doctor Clark
imploring you to have Pfizer vaccines

school photo of you twelve eyes blue from belt
of father mother brothers their orders

of service portraits of you cradling Con
me floating Mum on your wedding day snaps

of Con bearing two kids me hugging books
Mum jiving with girlfriends unused condoms

no coins passport lottery ticket torch
I throw in your towel wonder if you did

WHITE HART LANE, 12TH SEPTEMBER 2021

Love Lane Estate blocks—the distant siblings
passing shadows amongst their guests.

> Past shadows are amongst their guests.
> St. Paul's yutes are outdoors kicking bricks.

A soot-pulled rain kicks against outdoor bricks,
melts them to crumbs atop pavement.

> Man's out picking crumbs atop pavement,
> picks up a rusted pound coin.

If he trusts that this pound coin
isn't the broken promise of the last one,

> then this promises to be the last one
> before man hauls himself from Whitehall Street,

before man holds hall parties on white streets—
Love Lane Estate blocks, the distant siblings.

MENTAL HEALTH & EMPLOYEE WELLBEING LIAISON

to address the office's deteriorating mental health
they brought in a cuddle rhino
this animal was not tame it was fully grown
at first staff were shy about approaching its two-ton body
the rhino didn't appreciate attempts to cuddle
it preferred chasing them out of windows

eventually it emptied the office
the photocopier in pieces chairs sideways
paperwork wet on the street the staff

and management became concerned
about the rhino's own mental health
impacting his performance as an employee
their experts said
perhaps social anxiety perhaps a personality disorder
so they brought in a cuddly tarantula
to put on his head
which really made a difference
calmed him right down

THE SERMON OF SHRIPNEY LANE

Let it be known that in my former life
I curled like a pill bug or mothball
onto my parents' patching carpet.

In those days we learned to live with the darkness,
honoured its arrival as the lord of woodsmoke
that reigns over thatched burrows

and cross-stitched country lanes. In those days
we would provoke the fire that crackles like bubble wrap
and agitate the king of limbs in his cobweb court,

creep to the cross of the chicken coop and
kneel in confession to those barbed-wire bishops,
consecrating their patch of damp downland.

Father forgive this dwindling daylight
that paints patterns on chapel walls
like some sallow pastel or paste,

winter's wet dregs stirring birds
from the canopy or badgers from hedgerows.
This staircase doesn't creak like it used to,

and everything but the rain whispers silences
like prayers to household gods that
command woodworms from furniture
and march mice like soldiers
beneath furtive floorboards.

CINCINNATI UNION TERMINAL, SUMMER 1978
a golden shovel after czesław miłosz's child of europe

lies derelict. this poor man's st paul's, lost treasure
of rail lines, this cathedral god forgot, the whole of your
country, america, towering over my father. legacy
is a distant prospect. i am not yet a thought to this youth of
eighteen come across the atlantic to share his skills
in soccer, in pot-scrubbing, at a jewish boy's camp, child
teaching children, now abandoned to the calling of
all these great cities. america sprawls, is wide where europe
is old. dad seeks out history, catholic boy, inheritor
of every myth and shame. ohio names its largest, its home of
two million, twice for sin and like a magnet the gothic
calls him here. what does america know of cathedrals
but to build imitations of history? and here crumbling, shelter of
pigeons, the platforms excavated, gone to ruin, a baroque
basilica, its temple flanked by art deco angels. churches
are any place that welcomes a weary traveller, buildings of
song. pharoah sanders plays trackside, these synagogues
swelling with jazz and oh, the air, as he looks above, filled
with wings, balsa wood and tissue paper, rafters alive with
colour. he tells me that perhaps he dreamt it, flight like the
descent of leaves, and the shouts, cheering, wailing,
from above, parents and children, teachers and pupils, all of
them enraptured, racing model planes to the ground — a
moment lost to memory, until the radio dj wronged
it with a half-hearted description, void of life, void of people.

KEEP YOUR EYES ON THE ROAD

I want to experience true terror
in the passenger seat of your car

hitting 100
                 cruising motorway
                                   headed nowhere

an unknowable city
on either side.

Now

consider

at the end of the road:
white cliffs, dark night, the wind
rattles the barbed wire
of your chest hair, howling
the sound of a misunderstanding.

The feeling of a bruise
from an over-retched diaphragm,
a sky with the clarity
of a dream.

You are fixed
like I was, a child, to the blue
snow on the TV
almost crushing myself

when I tried to climb in
out here, there is still plenty
to climb through.
The caves in the cliffside carrying

generations of your family
trauma pouring into the skin.
This really is a cold,
cold night.

You, shaved to the scalp
missing your steel —
do you exit into the night
as a wound, or

do you slash the air
your arm a scalpel, climb through

almost crushing yourself.

STOPPING BY THE LOVE HOTEL

Whose rooms these are I think I know.
Viol & thigh high through window glow.
Coffee powder, blue teletext, Asahi beer.
Two beds * wink ;) * aesthetically rococo.

It seems I am happiest when I am here
at the window – red sky – far & clear.
Between these sheets to dream & wake
where it is far warmer with lovers near

& nails of mauve & glittering fake
turning the shower head for a break
to hot water falling beside the sink
& when we leave – the bed we make.

In the corridor now tinged with pink
you whispering softly as one last kink
the hotel was lovely, don't you think?
the hotel was lovely, don't you think?

WATERGATE BAY HOTEL

I ordered a sticky toffee pudding in a shiny blue bowl   took
it up to the room at the top
let   the ice cream melt and float like petrol   just me and
the duvet
a new sheet and my body tucked under it   and I rubbed my feet
back together
and let a comedian keep me company on the little telly in the corner
    and I was glad
not to have to be anywhere   or anyone's   and the sea
got darker I got stiller
and I can't remember leaving the bowl or the spoon but it greeted me in
the morning   sides
going hard on the grey bedside like cold sand drying in the bright —
                                    Everyone's favourite Sunday weather
        everyone out there already
        when the morning knocked the door   I laid there the same
way lovers do
                            pulling the other one back to bed as the shower
calls their warm bodies in —

SWIM

When my pastel-coloured swimming costume started to wear away at the
chest
it told my legs to keep on swimming   to be flecks
of 80s confetti and prick the man who
          called them *pins*

          nice pins he kept saying from the window of the plastic barber
shop
          the bus stop   the supermarket floor.

          I swam past them all
the little men

                              got stuck in the filter
like they told me I would with all my hair
my fake glow fell away
I swam past the prom dress on the hanger
and through the turnstile at Loftus Road
                    this time not like an animal waiting   half
finished to be told
                    not to dilly-dally   or that I had
bedroom eyes
but to kick back
past all the perfect people in perfect towns
          who weren't perfect and nor was their town —
past the commuters who shouted *sack the juggler!*

          I left them to clumsily drag themselves home plastered
and I swam past the road

where women take their joy out with the bins
past the chippy   and the bikes   the barman who asked me to
stay
past the local who asked what my real job was as he highlighted the tv
guide
            and I thought about my Mum   all those years
and her heart

a big octopus of a thing

that was inked to see what was going on with it
            and mine kept on floating
so I kept on going
                              past the girls who threatened to drown me
            past the big brick they kept making us dive down for
I took off my cap
            and I swung it
                  and my hair was whiter than the tiles' shine

                  I climbed out   of the chlorine
the legs of the mums in the gallery café all cheered
                                          and I was the
most upright thing —

THIS TIME LAST YEAR

Ok so there's a sea &
I'm inside it
Bobbing like a chew toy
On the dashboard
It's so beautiful here I might die
I used to cycle to the waves & think
I could take that
My mum has an app that she trusts more
Than her eyes
Tells her: 43 wind / 55 gust / 6-10 surf
Sucks her teeth in
Her wetsuit coiled in a bag for life
By the flask, the flapjack
But I'm inside the sea now
& all the fish are dead & the kelp is dead
& there's a windfarm 13 miles away but
I haven't got my badge yet so
Yeah, I'm intimidated
I look at a flat on the promenade &
Imagine all the water inside
The jars of brine for winter, rough salt in a tiny bowl
I've spent too long here
I've waded outside my context
The sun's setting
A colleague asks me how I got where I am
In some large city that has only ponds & puddles
I say I'm confused, all this liquid in my pocket
I'm leaking & he frowns, swirls a cloth around his glasses
It was so hard to get out

You lose your legs after a while, your hair mats

Your fat has to guide you to shore, like a lantern, a satsuma

Down the staircase

I want to be clear; she was generous

How she threw me to the pebbles. The pubs with their

Amber glow, under the starlings & the seagulls

Spit me out, I said

And she did

GROWING UP IN MOSH PITS

You, the boy who
never knowingly danced,
asked *how do you*
protest, is it still the same?
Your body statue still.
Clutching yourself
harder than you allow
yourself be held. Left leg
pulsing the bassline, ass
jerking. Mostly all of the
following. Silent. Whole.
Still. Remedial frozen
peaceful. Mostly.
Do you still rub scars,
caution stuck to your
shoulder till the beat
forms up your thigh
& insinuates itself till
your back spasms & you
move eyes closed, left arm
hanging sloppy as you
allow yourself to be
slowly taken over? Left
hand miserable, traces
an arc. Your body
satellites. You are
pointing at something &
it sure ain't the song. You
find you lost yourself

too early, committed to
the movement of gone.
Find your arm is carrying
the motion & your body
following suit,
straitjacket. This is
an orbit encore isn't it?
Silhouette of community
thrown onto the wall.
Shapes terse, identity of
shadows skewed by
the light of everyone's
blocking their own light
till the song leaves
grateful but never
knew when to stop,
meteor of understanding
body's spins. There's a
gravity to all this closure.
Hobby horse body
let yourself be pushed,
the edges are only
dangerous if no one pulls
you back. No one with a
known name to the
front, camaraderie of
violence. The gestalt of
shove. There seems to be
an equilibrium of other

people. If violence has
enclosed you-you can't be
the target. You reach for
the mic, your body
swollen by everyone else
making the same motion.
How can you be
so clumsy & intricately
choreographed as this?
How can this be
anything else other than
language? Dance, bitch.
Do you still collapse?
Boy of no rhythm, take
your clay mouth from
the chorus. In
the moment you'll find
forgiveness for thinking
they really care about you
& all that you truly are. A
mosh pit is a bruise
permitted by the
willing. Rationing the
chipped tooth, beside
yourself that someone
may be watching as you
miss the step, & your eyes
closed & you can't
see them seeing you.

ON RECEIVING NEWS FROM DERBY OF MY MOTHER'S DEATH WHILE LEADING AN ARCHAEOLOGICAL TOUR OF A VILLAGE IN MESOPOTAMIA

I was six-fields far when the news came.
A boy, barefoot and breathless,
found me, near the dried-up riverbed.
He had a minor official's joy of importance:
hanging on, expecting a tip for his trouble,
his dusty, cracked feet and impossible nylon shorts,
shadowing my movements.

Ölmüş, he said,
and within these words,
the world became flatter in the heat,
and the slim half pennies of shadows and shade were spent in an instant,
and the beetles, busying to hide from the weight of the day,
dropped through cracks in the earth,
straight into the Derwent and the Dove,

and, in spite of the bright linens of the group in front of me,
my mind blanched everything
into the brightest green of a Derbyshire evening,
with petrichor singing Methodist hymns from the hills above the town,
and the heat of '76, having flayed my shoulders,
went skulking, late in the day, to the bottoms of hedges,
and my mother, a goddess in white flared trousers,
held my hand as I balanced on the pub car park wall.

I saw her, tucked into the last remaining shade,
at the bottom of the burial mound,
knee-high in Anatolian fat-tailed sheep,

shooing them to spread a blanket,
pouring dandelion and burdock into beakers as a treat,
and telling me childhood tales of the snow of '46,
of gated roads, and of Monday's market, and of grace before tea:
the lodgers with butter, and she, always unhappy with hand-me-downs.

I didn't stop the tour, the news hidden by sleight of language,
the single mosaic square I'd been holding,
still in my hand, as I talked through
dams and droughts and deserted Roman baths
and days of water buffalo and wheat and the power of the diviner,
and while the circle of bucket hats, entitled and elegant,
nodded over pottery and pressed on,
debating how a Roman Bath could have ever been in this dust bowl,
she stood nodding to me,
not breaking sweat in the heat.

PENNY BINOCULARS, WESTON-SUPER-MARE, 1973

It trickled shoeward, tracing known highways
of traumas, scars and sores; my legs a maze
of shame — a bully's playtime paradise
of fun. I tried to stop, to squeeze my thighs,
already hearing Mother sigh, *Again?*
Your gusset's always soaking, filthy, stained.
At Sunday school, the sea was stopped with ease,
and me, the sinner, unable to halt even this.

The pier too long, the reason I'd come, a dot
away at the end. The man next door had held
my hand inside his hand, money inside
that, squeezing tight, promising I'd enjoy it.
The penny was sweating, stuck in my palm like guilt:
a tinny blood-smell, mixing with sea salt.

TYNE COT CEMETERY

The farmers are accustomed to sifting
bones and teeth from their peaceful pastures –

the same their ancestors saw overturned.
They saw men swallowed without a name or age,

far from a mother's prayer and lover's embrace.
Liberated from fear and choking

on mud and horsehair and flesh of comrades
and enemies alike, shrapnel hacking at throats

never shaved, rifles strapped across twisted spines
built by mothers' hands at home. Never fired.

For all they sought to end the suffering,
they couldn't pull the trigger.

For what's the use of ending slaughter
by putting a bullet in the head of a boy

different only by flag.

GRASS FIRE

Reminded of what in Wanstead Flats
catches light and stays alight
below the surface and will not stop.

I remember smaller fires
in childhood's summer heat.
It was not unusual to see smoke,
to know the flats had caught again
and afterwards to walk there, find and follow
the drastic mottle charred brushless and black.

But there had been no blaze before like the blaze
which took hold on Wanstead Flats five years ago.
One noon during that heatwave we stepped out
to meet grass smoke, the bouquet of seared trees,
and later saw a fan of smoke loom slant
on the bare sky, received the acrid thumbprint
to the back of the throat; and it was clear
this fire was not to be like other fires.

I could not take my usual route to work.
Those roads in Aldersbrook were cordoned off
and evacuated. I approached a fiasco
on Blake Hall Road. The fire
had squared up to their garden fences,
snarled at bedroom windowsills;
great combs of flame at it;
the gorse and broom had gone up brilliant,
and bushes were reduced to cinder skeletons.

On Dames Road I watched long billows lean
on the air, indicating their cryptic *qiblas*.
Beyond a bright band seethed,
the restless fire hard at dispassionate work
resisting the thick water cords cannoned
in high arcs, crisscross, from firefighters' firehoses.
And momentarily I thought of a million beetles
burning and the curled worm brittling to dust;
then, how the fire would leave vast black scars,
near naked ash and earth; no scrub remains
uncharred in those swept zones.

When at last the fire was quelled
and we could go on Centre Road again,
I went on Centre Road and marvelled
at the great swathes of it:
the remainder, pared, black and simpering,
stubbled by the somehow still-there
weak gold tufts and weak gold stumps.
Whereas the fires of my childhood would mark
the flats here and there, this less governable
fire had left huge stretches defaced.
I watched arcing spouts still dousing
the ground, the submerged peat smouldering on,
but these spouts leapt and swung unattended
from that same blistered dirt. The cindery air
touched tenderly the back of my throat,
the thumbprint's bullseye.

Reminded of that episode. A thumbprint
in the mind imparts a vision of multifid flames
shuddering and leaping between stripped trees;

a WhatsApp message from a woman I knew
then, new here and here temporarily;
and grassland blasted in unmeaning shapes.

A GROUP OF BURNING PEOPLE DISCUSS WHY THEY'RE ON FIRE

trade fault like property, confess
flood, the way a river confesses
its banks,

           mouths, the shape of birds
throwing themselves against glass

reciting the wrong alphabet,

                here,

                          the second A
the chance to begin again

you're not hollow,

           you're full of sky.

FEBRUARY IN SCARBOROUGH

The sun rose that morning like a molten orb
Birthed from my dirty sea,
Silhouetting a thousand gulls as they took flight from the tops of crumbling
Victorian hotels.
The crescent moon bay, not yet aware of itself,
Cupped the encroaching brine like a crooked hand
Willing time and tide to reach a little higher and finish their endless work.
An old woman in a purple velvet coat
Wanders past Salvation Lane,
Talking loudly to herself about some distant injustice
"It's the law, it's fair"
She shouts as the fruit machines in Wetherspoons are powered up.
Dogs have colonised the beach now,
Frantically chasing balls that bounce like subatomic particles,
Never sure which is the one they're running for.
Three children dig a hole, flicking restlessly through the flat sand,
Brows furrowed and aiming only down.
In the water you strive to find the wave that will carry you upright and home,
While I search for treasures to show you when your two hours have worn out
And breathe in vinegar and salt and brick dust.

SONNET FOR WIMPEY FIELD

Back then, I was still boyish—flat chest to match. The goal
-posts on Wimpey field are rusty staples stamped into a verdant page.
My friends and I would hang limp from the crossbar: a drooping
washing line of Liverpool FC shirts donned by lads from East Hull.
As kids, we'd climb a nearby beech tree with post-match panting,
chests heaving, the bark greased by mud on our boots.
Five years on, the stubborn sludge before each post is untouched.
No stud marks peppering the ground like misfired artillery, no footballs
pelted toward the crossbar, no metal twang echoing in the air. Instead, a stench
seeps through the soil. When I go to climb the beech for old times' sake, I stop
in my tracks. Unhook my foot from a branch. Larvae squirm in the stump,
the trunk ripped open like a wound, like a mouth mid-death rattle. I walk home,
mourn mud-flecked memories. Leave the past in the past. Sometimes,
it is better not to go back.

THE TEAROOM OF DISCONTENT

Mary had this dream.
A bell above the door,
the menu on chalkboard,
warm scones and homemade lemonade.
Ludlow, that would work,
or somewhere in Somerset.
Traditional in style, but welcoming
to all types of people.

The years drifted and the dream did too.
Rising interest rates, her sciatica,
her husband's recalcitrance
and new electric bike, the *cunt*,
but she kept her plans in her breast pocket
on carefully folded notepaper,
patted the thick wadge for comfort
when life throbbed like a hip.

After wine with dinner
or a brandy in the bath,
the dream could feel more vivid,
the sketched outlines ink-rich in her mind.

One day she told the girls at quilting group,
frothed foolishly about cakes, sandwich fillings,
the best choice of font for the sign.
Meryl smiled and nodded but
group-leader Shirley told her things had moved on,
no one drinks tea anymore,

it's all nut milk and goji-berries
according to her granddaughter,
who only eats herbs and thinks
sandwiches are homophobic.

Shirley's dream came true years ago,
back before all her facelifts
and now she sits there smug,
caressing her ugly cat's belly
while nansplaining backstitch to the group.

Mary limped home in the mizzle,
aware that she should probably phone
her busy son in Melbourne
but also aware that
she couldn't be fucked.

Months later, her breast pocket reached capacity,
stuffed to bursting with costings and sketches.
In the garden that night,
she set the lot on fire.
She warmed her stiff hands
on her dream set alight,
considering what to burn next.

Maddy Accalia (she/they) is a writer from Brighton, based in South London. Her plays have been performed at the Roundhouse, Vault Festival, Gilded Balloon, North Wall and Norwich Theatre Royal Stage 2. She was a Roundhouse Resident Artist from 2021-2023 and is currently writing her first novel.

Zahra Leyla Ahmad is a London-based poet and writer. She is fascinated by intersectionality and how this shapes her identity, navigating life as a Muslim British-Bangladeshi woman of colour. She has featured at Write2Speak, Deen & Dunya, Mehfil, and Mayor of London's Eid in the Square with WAW Creative Arts.

Dean Atta is an award-winning Black British author and poet of Greek Cypriot and Jamaican heritage. He is the author of *I Am Nobody's Nigger*, *The Black Flamingo*, *Only On The Weekends*, *There is (still) love here*, *Confetti*, and *Person Unlimited*. Dean lives in London.

Adam Barrett is a writer from Northumberland who lives in County Durham. His work explores class, mental health, and masculinity through the lens of the post-industrial North East landscape. Broken Sleep Books will release his debut pamphlet in August 2025.

Laurie Bolger is a London based writer & founder of The Creative Writing Breakfast Club. Laurie's work has featured at Glastonbury, TATE & Sky Arts. Laurie was awarded the The Moth Prize & was shortlisted for The Sylvia Plath, Bridport & Forward Prizes. Her latest books *Makeover* & *Spin* celebrate her working class Irish heritage.

Cogwheel is an artist, writer and musician who lives (and grew up) in the rural outskirts of Stoke-on-Trent. With uncounted years' experience of chronically successful hoarding, Cogwheel continues to live life as somewhat of a recluse, collecting and writing in an attempt to capture fleeting and sometimes festering thoughts with words and song.

Ella Dorman-Gajic is a writer, performer, producer and facilitator working across theatre, poetry, and screen. She is the co-founder, host and producer of Off The Chest. Ella's work has been described as "impassioned" by *The Guardian*. An alumna of Roundhouse Poetry Collective and Apples &

Snakes Writing Room, her poetry has been broadcast on BBC Radio and published in *Poetry Wales, Ink, Sweat and Tears, Zindabad Zine,* and more. Her work has been performed across the UK, including a tour of her 5-star stage play Trade (published with Salamander Street), which sold out at Pleasance and Norwich Arts Centre. Her multi-award-winning short film, *Back of the Net,* has screened at multiple BIFA-accredited festivals. She can be found between Peckham streets and Brighton shores.

Rick Dove is a progressive poet and activist from South London. Published in anthologies, zines, and journals since 2016, Rick also has two solo collections with Burning Eye Books; *Tales From the Other Box* (2020), *Supervillain Origin Story* (2023) and was crowned UK Poetry Slam Champion in 2021.

Laurie Eaves is a poet from the village of Yapton, living in London. His collection, *Biceps,* is out on Burning Eye. His work has been published by Bad Betty Press, *Ink Sweat & Tears* and *Atrium Poetry* amongst others. He co-hosts the *Dead Darlings* podcast and produces Genesis Poetry Slam.

Sam J Grudgings is a queer horror poet, storyteller & events host from Bristol, shortlisted for the Out-Spoken Poetry Prize 2020. His debut collection *The Bible II,* was released by Verve Poetry Press in 2021. His pamphlet *The Nation's Saddest Love Poems* was published in 2023 with Broken Sleep Books.

Marianne Habeshaw is a queer poet from Peterborough, currently living in London. She is a Barbican Young Poet (2023 & 2024) the founder of 'Thoughtcast Collective,' and was highly commended in the Outspoken Page Poetry Prize. She has upcoming anthology publications with Flipped Eye.

Oli Isaac is a London-based playwright and poet who likes to write tender poems about their tender thoughts. Oli is a recipient of Audible Theatre's Emerging Playwrights Fund and most recently the winner of the 2024 Verve Poetry Festival Competition.

Arun Jeetoo is an educator, facilitator, performer and writer from London, UK. His debut pamphlet *I Want to Be the One You Think About at Night* is published by Waterloo Press (2020). Instagram @g2poetry.

Rachel Jeffcoat is a Hampshire-based poet whose work has appeared or is forthcoming in a variety of publications, including *Atrium, Under the Radar, Tears in the Fence, New Welsh Review* and *The Interpreter's House*. Her first pamphlet, *Moult*, was recently shortlisted for publication by the Emma Press.

Joshua Jones is a queer, neurodivergent writer & artist from Llanelli, South Wales. He co-founded Dyddiau Du in Cardiff, a library and artspace led by and for LGBTQ+ and Disabled communities. *Local Fires* (Parthian Books, 2023) is his first book, and was recently shortlisted for the Dylan Thomas Prize.

Jonathan Kinsman is a trans poet, living in the wilds of the Hope Valley in the Peak District. He is a slam champion and his debut collection *The Fireman's Daughter* was published by Broken Sleep Books in 2023. Find him online @ manykinsmen.

Christopher Lanyon is a poet and mathematician from Cornwall, living in Nottingham. His poems have appeared in *Brittle Star, HAD, Ambit, Abridged, SPOONFEED, Finished Creatures & Under the Radar*, among others. His debut pamphlet, *swell*, is available from Bad Betty Press.

Iftikhar Latif is a writer and poet of British-Bangladeshi descent from East London. His work often refers to the British Asian experience, immigrant family relationships, deconstructions of masculinity, media culture and growing up in the city. He is co-founder, host and producer of Off The Chest. He has worked with the V&A for their 2022 'Drip Maketh the Man' project, the Apples and Snakes 2022 Writing Room and was a resident poet at The Sidings in Waterloo Station in 2024.

Len Lukowski is a writer and performer based in Glasgow. His work has been published in *Extra Teeth, New Writing Scotland* and elsewhere. His debut pamphlet, *The Bare Thing* was published in 2022 by Broken Sleep Books. He is the winner of the Wasafiri 2018 New Writing Award for Life Writing.

Alex Mazey won The Roy Fisher Prize from Keele University in 2018 and was the recipient of a Creative Future Writers' Award the following year. He is the author of *Living in Disneyland, Sad Boy Aesthetics*, and *Ghost Lives: Cursed Edition*.

James McDermott is a Norwich based writer. Poetry collections include *Wild Life* (Nine Arches Press), *Erased* (Polari Press) and *Manatomy* (Burning Eye). Plays published by Samuel French include *Jab* (Finborough Theatre), *Time & Tide* (Park Theatre) and *Rubber Ring* (Pleasance). James writes on *EastEnders* and lectures in scriptwriting at UEA.

Jay Mitra (they/he) is a British Indian punk poet and creative non-fiction writer from Hull, now based in London. Currently, he is pursuing a career in teaching and working as a freelance writer and facilitator. You can find out more about them on Instagram and Twitter @punkofcolour.

Francis-Xavier Mukiibi is a poet of Ugandan heritage from North London. He is a Barbican Young Poets, Roundhouse Poetry Collective and Obsidian Foundation alumnus. His poems have appeared in *Ink Sweat & Tears, Under the Radar, Propel Magazine, Poetry Wales, Broken Sleep Books* and *Flipped Eye* among others.

Molly Naylor is an award-winning poet, scriptwriter, and graphic novelist. She is the co-writer and creator of Sky One comedy *After Hours.* Her plays have been toured nationally and broadcast on BBC Radio 4. Her third poetry collection *Whatever You've Got* is published by Bad Betty Press.

George Neame is a poet and publisher from West Sussex, now based in London. His pamphlet *The Infinite Flood* was published by Broken Sleep Books in 2023 and his poetry has appeared in *Acumen, The Moth* and *The Interpreter's House* among others.

James O'Hara-Knight is a writer from East London. He has had poems highly commended in the Live Canon International Poetry Competition and the Winchester Poetry Prize. His writing has been shortlisted and longlisted in other prizes, and appears in anthologies and journals. He currently tutors, but for three years he was a secondary school librarian in Ilford.

Rhiya Pau is a poet of Indian heritage from a community with a rich history of migration. Her debut poetry collection, *Routes*, won a 2022 award from the Society of Authors. She previously won the 2021 Creative Future Writers' Award and a commendation in the 2023 Forward Prizes. Rhiya currently splits her time between London and San Francisco.

Kari Pindoria is a writer from North London. Her poetry has been previously published in *And Other Poems, Propel, Unbroken journal* and *Ink, Sweat and Tears.* You can find her on Twitter @karipindoria.

Ankita Saxena is a London-based writer and performer. Her debut poetry collection, *Mother | Line*, released in April 2023 with Verve Poetry Press – a culmination of over a decade of writing, editing and performing. She is one half of South Asian poetry duo Origins, and a former Barbican Young Poet.

Harry Slater is a queer writer based in the East Midlands, on a tract of flood plain next to the River Derwent. They were raised in a corner of the north that's being reclaimed by the sea.

Jack Solloway is a writer from the West Midlands living in London. His poems have appeared in *Poetry Wales* and *Poetry Birmingham Literary Journal.* His latest poetry pamphlet, *SERIOUSLY,* is out now with Broken Sleep Books.

Yago Soto-André is a poet, freelance creative, community support worker and gardener based in London. His poems have been featured in magazines and anthologies, including *Propel Magazine, And Other Poems* and in *Masculinity: An anthology of Modern Voices,* as well as being shortlisted for the 2023 Out-Spoken Page Poetry Prize.

Lalah-Simone Springer (she/they). Lalah is a poet and speculative fiction writer from Dagenham, currently living in Newham. Their debut poetry collection, *An Aviary of Common Birds* was published in 2023 alongside their collaborative spoken word album, *Cyclical Music.* Previous collaborations as a performance artist have been staged at The Barbican, Whitechapel Gallery, and Folkstone Fringe.

Sophie Sparham is a poet and writer from Derby. They have written commissions for BBC Radio 4, The V&A and The People's History Museum. They host the night Word Wise which won best spoken word night at the 2019 Saboteur Awards. Their latest collection *The Man Who Ate 50,000 Weetabix* came out in April 2021 via Verve Poetry Press.

Alison Tanik is a poet, performer and playwright from Derby. She's currently doing her masters in poetry at MMU. Alison won the DPF East Midlands Prize 2023 and was commended for the Verve Poetry Festival Prize 2023. She performs her poetry at gigs nationwide as Who the Fuck is Alice.

Laura Tansley is originally from Malvern in the West Midlands. Her collection of visual poetry, *Notes to Self*, was published by Trickhouse Press. Her co-written collection of short fiction with Micaela Maftei, *The Reach of a Root*, was published by Vagabond Voices. She lives in Glasgow.

INTERVIEW WITH THE EDITORS

Below, Cia Mangat (founder of Zindabad zine and cover designer for this anthology) speaks to the editors Aaron Kent (Broken Sleep Books) and Jake Wild Hall (Bad Betty Press).

CIA: To start off with, I thought I'd be quite boring and ask you to talk me through your experience of editing the anthology.

JAKE: In terms of just putting the anthology together, it's been wonderful to get to work with Aaron and to work with Off The Chest. I think me and Aaron's symbiosis in getting the work we wanted and the feel of it has been great. And we felt very supported by Off The Chest. And I think the anthology is something that pays tribute to the community of Off The Chest. Which was super important in this because it's not just an anthology edited by me and Aaron, it is obviously the first ever Off The Chest anthology, who have such a rich history and a strong community that we wanted to honour that as well.

AARON: And something that's interesting for me is that the poems have to be designed to be read on the page, but also read aloud as part of a performative act. So when looking for these poems, I knew any changes that I suggested were going to affect the performance, but maybe I can make a suggestion that is going to bring out the performance. And it's kind of learning to balance both the performative tendency for work while also ensuring that it works as a statement on the page.

CIA: That's kind of tricky to balance, isn't it? I think I've been to a couple of Off The Chest events over the years. And one thing I love about the open mic is that you don't really know what you're getting. It feels almost randomly generated based on whose name gets picked out. I think that eclectic-ness is at the heart of the Off The Chest community. How do you bring that to an anthology?

AARON: Something I learned is that you have to trust the poet when it comes to performance. The majority of poets I have published, seem to read quite well. But I have come across some published poets whose work I have been really excited by and then heard them read and think: 'oh, you don't know how to read your own work... You've spent so long writing your poetry, that you've forgotten how to speak your poetry.' And it's always a shame. I always want to say to poets, when you've written a book, spend time learning to read your own work because otherwise the performance is the same as reading the book. So you kind of have to trust that the poets know what they're doing. I find that if there's energy in the words on the page, then I can have faith that there'll be energy in the words on the stage. It's like they say, energy in the sheets = energy on the streets!

JAKE: I think in terms of eclectic-ness as well it is worth saying that poetry isn't just "one thing is good, one thing is bad". What makes a poem wonderful is a big spectrum of things right? And so sometimes things can be very high literature, and you can love that. And I quite like literary stuff (my favourite author is Max Porter). But also, I love just some good old spoken word. You know, I mean, I can't tell you how many times I've watched Jessica by Polarbear. So when we read stuff, when we're trying to get that eclectic balance, we might pick something that we know is very, very good that isn't quite 10 out of 10. Like, God, damn, this is so well crafted. This is so good but it might not hit you. It might not emotionally be something that hits you. But you have an understanding of why it is fantastic.

CIA: I'm also thinking of the broadness of the poems. When I was reading through the submissions, that broadness is reflected not just in the way people are writing, but also in how they approach the theme. I wonder if you could talk a bit more about that?

JAKE: I think with any theme, what's good is to have enough poems that are really rooted in a core understanding of that thing. So it's obvious what that place of significance is, e.g. my grandma's house, Cyprus, etc. Do you know what I mean? And then it can be more ethereal. And it's good to pick something because it has such a good connection to the theme. You need a few of those. You have to pick some that are really based in the theme and have done the work of that, specifically so people can understand it. Aaron, would you agree with that?

AARON: I also think with themes, there's a difference between a theme which is intended to be ambiguous and a theme that is intended to be specific. So Broken Sleep have got an anthology coming out called *Devastation Songs*, and it's an anthology about giant monsters. Kaiju, Godzilla, all that stuff because I'm a massive Godzilla fan. For that anthology, if you're sending me a poem that has nothing to do with monsters and you've been really ambiguous, you're probably not gonna get in. However, when we did a masculinity anthology, where it was about what it means to be masculine in an age where we can be free from the toxicity of masculinity, how you write about that is more ambiguous. That's a different story to tell. And so that's why I think there's specific anthologies and there's ambiguous anthologies. And even ambiguous ones, if it's about place, for example, it still has to work. But you get more room to move. And then it's the editor's job to make sure that the theme flows while allowing that ambiguity to still exist.

CIA: Maybe this one is too wanky, but I'll ask you anyway. I was thinking about Off The Chest as like a space in and of itself, from having these performance nights across London and across the UK even. And the anthology is kind of like a portable space of significance. If the anthology was a space, what would the vibes in there be?

AARON: So I don't know if many people realise this about me as a poet. But I started as a spoken word poet. I started in slam. And I did it in various venues, I remember there was like, one which was in a bar in Falmouth on top of an already existing bar. And it had college students, it had people who would perform for years and knew the grasp of it, it had people who have never performed before but were doing it for the first time. There was a friend of mine who was like this emo kid, he was doing some hardcore emo stuff. But then there was also this guy from South Africa who was doing what felt like vocalisation of hip hop. And it had everything you want from a space, not just poetically and performatively, but also in terms of its social and cultural dynamic. And I think that's what we wanted to achieve with this anthology, which was to make a space where you can go "these are people I'd want to hang out with at a party" or even just sit with them and have them tell me their stories in a coffee shop. And that's what the anthology feels like to me.

JAKE: Listen, let's just leave it there. That's a 10 out of 10 answer. Next question.

CIA: One final quick question. I'm aware that many of the people reading this anthology may be starting out in the world of poetry, and may want to get their poems published for the first time or perform for the first time. As editors, do you have any top tips that you can offer someone who is picking this up and thinking, "you know what, I'm gonna do it. I'm gonna start sharing my work with people"?

JAKE: Just do it. I've got into a new process this year for the first time ever. So I have been writing and performing for 15 years, which seems like forever and ever. And it's only taken me until like my 30s to really start submitting poems and believing they're good enough. I wish I could take my younger self aside and just be like, do it. Every time you get a rejection, send a poem out, no matter what. Every time you get a rejection, send the poem out, go to nights, get the feel of them, get the smell of them, and make those connections. The early part of a poetry journey is the best because you're going to open mic nights and you're making friends and you're making the connections you'll have for the rest of your life and you're having a pint and you're doing your poem for the first time and you're meeting audiences. Just do as much as you can. Get involved. Go to open mic nights, go to slams, read poems, read online magazines, do it all and do it because you love it. And do it because this is what you want to do, and not because you think you're suddenly going to be the next Kae Tempest.

This interview has been slightly edited for brevity.

ACKNOWLEDGEMENTS

First and foremost, thank you to HiLand Cafe – Peter and Michael – for providing a space for our first-ever poetry events. Thank you to everyone working at the spaces we've filled: The Albany and Deptford Lounge, Canada Water Theatre, The Questors, Rich Mix, Omnibus, Hyde Park Book Club, Komedia Brighton, and Julia Bruns for bringing us to All Points East In the Neighbourhood Festival. Massive thanks to our assistant producers RubyK and Amelia Tan, as well as our resident DJ Lili Chin. We couldn't have done this without Aaron Kent and Jake Wild Hall, who guided us through the minefield that is publishing a poetry anthology – thank you. Thank you to Arts Council England for making this anthology possible. Finally, thank you to all our audiences, open mic'ers, participants and supporters over the years (you know who you are). We are not Off The Chest without you.

LAY OUT YOUR UNREST

www.ingramcontent.com/pod-product-compliance
Ingram Content Group UK Ltd.
Pitfield, Milton Keynes, MK11 3LW, UK
UKHW042335200625
459914UK00003B/107